THE ESSENTIAL
FAN GUIDE
BILLIE EILISH

MALCOLM CROFT

Bluestreak
BOOKS

CONTENTS

INTRODUCTION

BILLIE EILISH IS, QUITE SIMPLY, THE SOUND OF NOW. HER BODY OF WORK IN JUST A FEW SHORT YEARS IS PRECISELY HOW YOU EXPECT THE SECOND DECADE OF THE TWENTY-FIRST CENTURY— WITH ALL OF ITS FLAWS, FAILURES, AND FEARS—TO SOUND.

Without looking back at the past or apeing the sound of her peers, Billie is making thoroughly modern music that looks, feels, and sounds like no other artist around. In short, she has captured that creepy feeling we all sense in the world today and distilled it into creepy, freaky, utterly hypnotic—and yet strangely uplifting—music. The fact that Billie has yet to turn 20 years old is mind-blowing.

So many adjectives have been applied to Billie ever since she first appeared—strangely, magically, without warning—in 2015. And all of them are true. And false. Because none of them matter. Billie is Billie.

As we've come to discover about this singular shooting star, all that matters is being "what, and who, you want." From her fans and critics, Billie has won praise and adulation for her authenticity, for her confidence in her own creative vision, for the strength of her self-worth, and for not adhering to any rules, including her own. Even the behemoths of rock are behind Billie's ethos, citing her as a modern punk rebelling against everything—and nothing. "What I'm seeing happening with my daughters is the same revolution that happened to me at their age," Dave Grohl, legendary Nirvana drummer and Foo Fighters singer, said of Billie. "They're becoming themselves through her music." Radiohead's Thom Yorke agreed. "You're the only one doing anything . . . *interesting* nowadays," he told Billie. Finneas, Billie's brother, later described the comment to Billie as "the coolest thing anyone's ever said to you." It's not just cool—it's absolutely spot on.

With Billie's trippy, disjointed, and bleak take on all genres of music, and her baggy dress sense—"a collective middle finger to the strictures of teen-pop sex appeal," or just Billie dressing in what she feels comfortable, you decide—Billie Eilish may be different from any other pop star on earth, but she is no different from her fans. They are one and the same. She speaks for them and is with them. It's the Billie Eilish Paradox. The singer is a rebellious anti-hero and, conversely, also the safest role model around. Billie doesn't do drugs or drink, she doesn't sexualize her art or her body, and she wears her love for her family on her over-sized sleeves. She cares about her fans, yet she deliberately sets out to terrorize and petrify them. She looks terrifying, yet she stills jumps the last few feet into bed "in case there's a monster underneath waiting to grab her." Billie has conquered the music industry by doing everything she's not supposed to, which, paradoxically, will become the norm. But above all, Billie's global success is down to one simple truth: Billie is Billie. She does exactly what she wants her way. And you don't dare look away.

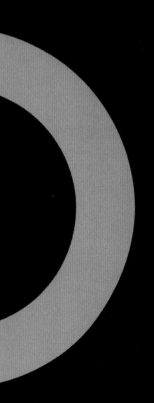

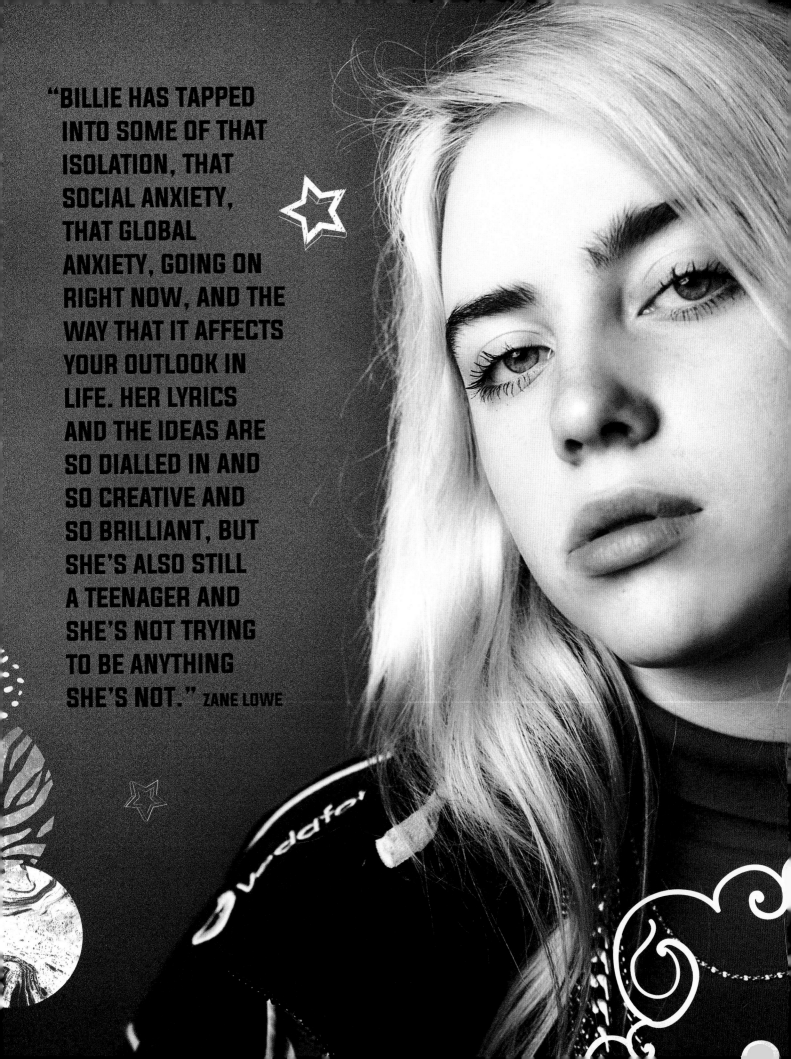

"BILLIE HAS TAPPED INTO SOME OF THAT ISOLATION, THAT SOCIAL ANXIETY, THAT GLOBAL ANXIETY, GOING ON RIGHT NOW, AND THE WAY THAT IT AFFECTS YOUR OUTLOOK IN LIFE. HER LYRICS AND THE IDEAS ARE SO DIALLED IN AND SO CREATIVE AND SO BRILLIANT, BUT SHE'S ALSO STILL A TEENAGER AND SHE'S NOT TRYING TO BE ANYTHING SHE'S NOT." ZANE LOWE

CHAPTER ONE

NO PLACE LIKE HOME

WHEN BILLIE EILISH RECORDED THE VOCALS FOR HER BROTHER'S HAUNTING POP BALLAD, "OCEAN EYES," AGED JUST 13, LITTLE DID SHE KNOW THE FUSS IT WOULD CAUSE. FIVE YEARS LATER, BILLIE'S BODY OF WORK TRANSCENDS GENRE, TASTE, AND AGE. THE SINGER NOW STANDS ON THE PRECIPICE OF BECOMING POP CULTURE'S MOST VALUABLE ASSET, AN ARTIST WHO REPRESENTS THE PERFECT MIRROR TO THESE DARK, TWISTED TIMES. BUT, NO MATTER HOW FAR BILLIE TRAVELS INTO THE POP STRATOSPHERE, HOME WILL ALWAYS KEEP HER FEET CONNECTED TO THE GROUND. "IT MADE ME WHO I AM. . . ."

In her journey from an unknown teenager to one of the world's most watched and most visually striking modern cultural icons, Billie has remained resolutely herself. Even her critics can't fault her fans' claim as the real deal.

Before Billie was born in Highland Park, a gritty neighborhood of Los Angeles, her parents, "unemployed" actors and musicians Maggie Baird and Patrick O'Connell, had been struggling to make ends meet. "People have a really weird interpretation of how I grew up, and I think it's because I'm a girl, I'm from LA, and an artist," Billie says of her upbringing. "Automatically, people think you're from Beverly Hills. Not at all. Highland Park has become popular now but growing up there, it was not like that at all . . . I couldn't go outside past dark because it was too dangerous . . . There were gunshots—a lot. "

When Billie arrived in December 2001, her parents had enjoyed walk-on parts in popular TV shows such as *Friends*, *Curb Your Enthusiasm*, and *The West Wing*. Both Maggie and Patrick were respected actors—Maggie was even a member of revered comedy troupe the Groundlings, with Will Ferrell, and was comedian Melissa McCarthy's first improvization teacher—but respect couldn't pay the bills. "I grew up with no money at all, I grew up poor. I had one pair of shoes and a shirt," recalled Billie. For Maggie and Patrick, fame always remained just around the

ABOVE Styled by American Outfitters, Billie attends the Teen Vogue Young Hollywood Gala, September 23, 2016.

LEFT An aerial view of Billie's home town—Highland Park, Los Angeles.

"PRETTY MUCH MY WHOLE LIFE I'VE BEEN A PERFORMER AND HAVE LOVED SINGING AND WRITING SONGS IN MY ROOM FOR MY OWN EARS. I NEVER THOUGHT A CAREER AS A MUSICIAN WAS POSSIBLE."

ABOVE A rare smile by Billie as she rocks up to the Teen Vogue Young Hollywood Gala, September 23, 2016.

corner. In the late 1990s, the couple decided to put their acting dreams on hold and instead dedicate their lives to becoming the best parents they could.

To do so, Maggie and Patrick filled the family home with music, sound, and color. And few rules. Home was a very small two-bedroom house, with Maggie and Patrick sleeping on a futon in the living room in order for Finneas and Billie to have their own bedrooms. Despite its petite size, the house had three upright pianos, one for every room.

"My whole family is really musical," Billie remembers. "My brother and my mom both write songs and my dad has always played the piano and ukulele. When we were little, my dad would make us mix tapes with songs by artists like the Beatles and Avril Lavigne, so we learned a lot from those." Indeed, the family even declared a rule: "We kind of had a rule in the house that no one would ever make you go to sleep if you were playing music," says Maggie, Billie's mom. "Music trumped everything."

With music forever swirling around their small home, the family became closer than most. It was between the hallway connecting the two children's bedrooms that Billie and her big brother by four years, Finneas, developed a chemistry that would form the basis of their songwriting success. On top of the family's dedication to music, Billie's parents believed that homeschooling was best for their children, a decision they made because Billie was a "sensitive child with severe separation anxiety"—anxieties that would build into other forms of mental health issues as Billie entered adolescence. Billie slept in her parents' bed until she was 10 years old. "One of us was with her literally around the clock," said Patrick. "Both kids were hard, but in different ways," recalls Maggie. "Finneas tortured you, but he was tortured himself, so you felt bad for him. Whereas

BILLIE'S YOUTUBE TOP 10

1. "BAD GUY" 2. "LOVELY" (WITH KHALID)
3. "WHEN THE PARTY'S OVER" 4. "BELLYACHE"
5. "BURY A FRIEND" 6. "OCEAN EYES"
7. "IDONTWANNABEYOUANYMORE"
8. "YOU SHOULD SEE ME IN A CROWN"
9. "ALL THE GOOD GIRLS GO TO HELL"
10. "MY BOY"

"I'M LUCKY TO HAVE A FAMILY THAT I LIKE, AND THAT LIKES ME. THE ONLY REASON I DO WHAT I DO IS BECAUSE MY PARENTS DIDN'T FORCE ME. IF THEY'D SAID, 'HERE'S A GUITAR, HERE'S A MICROPHONE, SING AND WRITE,' I WOULD HAVE BEEN LIKE, 'GOODBYE! I'M GOING TO GO DO DRUGS.'"

Billie enjoyed torturing you. She had no sympathy at all. She was like, 'Oh, you're crying? You're weak.'" "I was horrible," recalls Billie. "My goal was to get you to scream."

Homeschooling allowed the family to stay together, as well as giving Billie and Finneas the opportunity to indulge in their love of singing, dancing, and composing—subjects that they had expressed interest in since preschool. "I'm home-schooled and have been for my whole life," recalled Billie. "Instead of being forced to learn certain things in school that I won't really ever use in the world, I got to learn about things that I'm actually interested in and want to pursue. With everything happening with my music right now, being homeschooled has been really great."

While Finneas plonked himself down at the pianos and guitar, Billie's initial form of expression lay in ballet, tap, jazz, hip-hop and contemporary dance. And it was her love of dancing that ultimately led to her singing. "I was a dancer for a very long time, I should still be a dancer, but I got injured so I'm not," recalls Billie. "Dancing is what I thought I was really going to be focusing on. I was dancing eleven hours a week, recitals and all that. I mean dancing is what I thought I'd be doing, I kind of still am, because I dance when I'm on stage and I dance in videos and I want to have dancers eventually. I never really thought about having a 'job' job."

For several years Billie danced to her heart's content, even joining a competitive dance company. "That was probably

RIGHT Billie gate-crashes the premiere of *Everything Everything*, May 6, 2017. "Ocean Eyes" appears in the film.

when I was the most insecure," she recalls. "And I've never felt comfortable in really tiny dancer's clothes. I was always worried about my appearance. That was the peak of my body dysmorphia. I couldn't look in the mirror at all."

One day Billie's dreams of becoming a professional dancer quite literally crashed to the ground. "I was in a hip-hop class with all the seniors, the most advanced level, and I ruptured the growth plate in my hip." The injury meant she had to quit competitive dancing for good. That one truth destroyed her. She was 11. "I think that's when the depression started," Billie remembers. "It sent me down a hole. I went through a whole self-harming phase. I felt like I deserved to be in pain."

Haunted by the pain, frustration, and misery caused by that injury, Billie—with the help of therapy and her family—began to funnel her anxieties into songwriting, putting her tortured thoughts down on paper and setting them to chords. "I had all of this stuff in my head and I wanted to get it out," Billie said. "So I just wrote down all my thoughts and feelings and then made them into songs. There was no, 'I'm going to write a song now.' I just did it." Finneas, who himself was turning into quite an accomplished composer and lyricist at the same time as Billie,

was impressed with his little sister's initial efforts, even if their provenance was hardly mainstream pop.

Even though Billie never really thought of pursuing a job as a singer, she had always loved singing. "I was singing when I was coming out of my mother," she once joked. "I was always singing or making noise, always yelling, always listening to music. I had to be shushed sometimes—I would always make noise, which I still do."

To ensure Billie focused her singing energy into a constructive outlet, Maggie and Patrick signed Billie up to the Los Angeles Children's Chorus. It was there that she developed her now-famous voice. And learned how to use it. "I've been in the Los Angeles Children's Chorus since I was about eight. Everything that I use, I pretty much have learned from choir. It has helped my technique so much. It's showed me all of the different types of classic music there are and how beautiful they can be. When I was 11, I started writing songs because it's a good way to express your feelings. It also helped a ton with just learning how to play songs; I can kind of figure it out on my own. Choir has taught me the way to protect your voice . . . Some artists just ruin their voices because they don't know any better."

"ALL I'VE EVER WANTED IS TO BE ON A STAGE AND HAVE PEOPLE CHEERING FOR ME."

CHAPTER TWO

THE FAMILY BUSINESS

IT MAY BE BILLIE EILISH PIRATE BAIRD O'CONNELL'S MOUTHFUL OF A NAME YOU SEE UP IN LIGHTS, BUT BILLIE'S BRAND IS UNDENIABLY A FAMILY BUSINESS. IT COMES AS NO SURPRISE THEN THAT SHE CALLS HER LOYAL FANS "SIBLINGS," AND THAT ALL OF BILLIE'S AND FINNEAS'S ERA-DEFINING MUSIC WAS BORN OUT OF THEIR CHILDHOOD BEDROOMS.

When Billie began being viewed by the world's lens, she had only just turned 14. Maggie, her mom, was initially worried that fame would destroy her daughter's and son's ability to live free lives. Thankfully, due to the close-knit bond the O'Connells enjoy, Billie and Finneas are well equipped to deal with the pressures and expectations of super-fame. And the two siblings didn't have to travel far from home to change the world. The world came to them. For it was inside their childhood bedroom where their magic music first started to fuse. "People have put a lot of emphasis on our bedrooms as part of our lineage," remembers Finneas. (All of Billie's output to date has been created in the spaces of her and Finneas's bedrooms.)

ABOVE Billie and Finneas see red at the Life Is Beautiful Music Festival, Las Vegas, September 2019.

LEFT Mom Maggie, brother Finneas, and Billie at the Chanel J12 Yacht Club Dinner Event, July 2019. Billie and Finneas performed.

Hooks, lyrics, and melodies would ping between the two songwriters' adjoining rooms as they traded ideas. Finneas's room, where all the production occurred, is barely big enough to fit a bed, two keyboards, and a desk. And while it appears to be just the regular bedroom of a music-mad teenager, in essence, it remains the perfect representation of how pop music has changed in recent years.

No longer the domain of expensive studio sessions run by moguls and Svengalis, music is created, uploaded, and streamed in the bedroom. Billie said it best: "People always ask, 'How does it feel to have started out in your brother's tiny room, and now you're in the big studio?' But I'm not. I'm still in the same room." Today, after five years of hit-making, it's hard to imagine Billie and Finneas ever recording anywhere else. "I don't particularly like recording studios, they tend to be lifeless and without any natural light," said Finneas. "I'm sure Billie and I will start recording in my old room whenever we get back into recording mode for the next record. We don't want to be bound to a studio, who we'd have to pay untold sums to. Our mom lives in that house. Having your mom come in with delicious

food, telling you she loves your music, is a priceless confidence boost," he revealed. "That bedroom has a very specific sound too, very tight and intimate and closed and quiet. I love the way it makes vocals sound."

On the other side of the hall from her brother's "tiny-ass bedroom" lies Billie's domain.

Like many teenage girls, Billie's bedroom was (is, she still lives at home) her shelter. "My room is like my little palace," she revealed. "My room is the thing in my life that's changed the most over time. I change my mind a lot; my room has been twenty different rooms over the years."

Between the ages of 11 and 13, Billie began writing songs separately from Finneas, though her big brother would often hear sounds emanating from her bedroom that made him knock on her door. "The first time she sang [a song all the way through] she covered 'Hotline Bling' on a ukulele in our house," Finneas remembers. "I was like, 'Did you write this?' I believed it."

TOP Billie rocks the mic at Spotify's The Billie Eilish Experience. Mom Maggie and Finneas look on proud! Los Angeles, March 28, 2019.

LEFT Billie and Finneas show off their ASCAP Vanguard Award, presented to them by Oscar-winning actress (and Billie superfan!) Julia Roberts.

"I FEEL MYSELF LOSING IT A LITTLE, BUT I HAVE MY BROTHER. WE WRITE EVERYTHING TOGETHER; HE PRODUCES MY STUFF—AND MY MOM AND DAD TOUR WITH ME. WHEN I'M AWAY FROM HOME, AT LEAST I HAVE MY HOME WITH ME."

BELOW "They'll be here pretty soon, lookin' through my room for the money." Billie sings "Bellyache" at the Bonnaroo Music and Arts Festival, June 2019.

The siblings decided to join forces. "It was the beginning of 2015, we started writing together," remembers Billie. "We were three feet away from each other, what's the harm? We just did it, no expectations, no 'Let's do this to get this' or 'Let's get famous', whatever . . . Ours was just that we wanted to, we loved it, so we did."

Naturally, due to their bedrooms' proximity, being homeschooled, and having no parents telling them to keep their music down, Finneas and Billie were able to collaborate long and often. The fact that they were also each other's best friend made songwriting together even more productive. "We both take criticism really well. So he'll do something and I'll be like, 'No. That's terrible,' and he'll be like, 'Okay. You're right.'

And it's the same way with me. If I say, 'What about this?' he'll say, 'Nope,' because we can be honest. When you work with other people, you don't have that trust with them. So it's really easy. I get along really well with my brother, and I always have. We're really close. We're a team."

Despite the duo's ability to write songs together and know instinctively what the other was thinking, creatively, a decision was made fairly early on that they should never form a family band, even if Mom and Dad would often jam along. Today, Maggie and Patrick are happy to be tour and personal assistants, though Maggie is really more Billie's chief-of-staff, all mom and part manager, while dad assists with tour set design and, in the early days, chauffeuring.

LEFT Inseparable from a young age, Billie and Finneas have grown into a formidable songwriting duo.

BELOW Billie and her brother share vocal duties at a performance in Las Vegas.

Despite Finneas's and Billie's "unshakeable" bond, the siblings decided it was in the best interest of the music for them not to form a duo. "It was a deliberate decision to present everything under Billie's name," Finneas stated. "I don't think duos do very well. I can't think of a duo that has become as successful as Billie in today's climate. There are many duos that I love, but the press doesn't really know what to do with a duo, and also Billie is such an iconic-looking person, it felt right that it's her project."

With the two songwriters being gifted in their own separate ways, the pair acknowledge that they need each other—Billie's darkness balances out Finneas's lightness. And, ultimately, they are their own artists who have their own lives too. "We are both solo artists who make music together," says Finneas. "Billie's record is totally her creative vision. We make the music together, but she comes up with the album art and visual ideas, also for the live shows. For me, that's one of many reasons why it is her music."

Proud mom Maggie agrees. "Billie doesn't hold back on her opinions. She wants the creative to be what she wants it to be, and she has a vision and says what that is. She never goes along with something just to make it easier. Billie has a very clear vision, and when she expresses it, people move."

And move they did. With Finneas and Billie conjoined in their creativity, it didn't take long before the pair struck gold with a tune that was as big, blue, and as beautiful as its subject matter—"Ocean Eyes."

OPPOSITE Billie and Finneas pose for a family portrait at SXSW Festival, Austin, March 2017.

SPOTIFY CHART HISTORY*

Numbers represent streams. Billie has 46 million monthly users.

"BAD GUY" = 951,758,656

"LOVELY" = 734,084,534

"WHEN THE PARTY'S OVER" = 636,698,432

"BURY A FRIEND" = 512,284,945

"WISH YOU WERE GAY" = 293,867,806

"OCEAN EYES" = 287,972,160

"IDONTWANNABEYOUANYMORE" = 286,499,313

"YOU SHOULD SEE ME IN A CROWN" = 228,071,140   **"BELLYACHE"** = 182,024,587

"I LOVE YOU" = 168,932,471

*Up to November 18, 2019

CHAPTER THREE

SOUND AND COLOR

FOR THE O'CONNELL FAMILY, EVERYTHING CHANGED WITH "OCEAN EYES." QUITE LITERALLY OVERNIGHT. BILLIE AND FINNEAS WENT FROM BROODING BEDROOM BEGINNERS TO ERA-DEFINING GAME-CHANGERS. THERE WAS NO LOOKING BACK.

From the cramped confines of Finneas's bedroom, the haunting, atmospheric, and gorgeous song "Ocean Eyes" was crafted. As of late 2019, it had more than 180 million views on YouTube and had been streamed on Spotify more than a billion times. Finneas had written the song for his LA pop band, The Slightlys, but something about the track was missing. It needed another voice. A girl. "He came in my room and said, 'This is a song I wrote,'" Billie recalls, "and I was like, 'I know. I live next to you. I can hear it all happen.'" According to legend—well, Billie—Finneas "begged" his little sister to record the missing vocal part.

The pair spent a week recording and mastering the song. "We just sat in the room dancing to it," remembers Billie. "At the time I was going through something with a boy; he had dark-blue eyes and they looked like the ocean to me. I always thought about oceans when I looked in his eyes. But my brother wrote it and when he sang it for me the first time I thought, 'This is exactly how I'm feeling, how did you do that?' It was like Finneas

LEFT Billie stops by the Young Hollywood Studio for a chat in Los Angeles, September 2017.

ABOVE Billie goes green at the 2017 Glamour Women of the Year Awards in New York.

N° 837 N° 838 N° 839 N° 840 N° 841 N° 842 N° 843 N° 844 N° 845 N° 846 N° 847 N° 912 N° 913 N° 914 N° 915 N° 916 N° 917 N° 918

851 N° 852 N° 853 N° 854 N° 855 N° 856 N° 857 N° 858 N° 859 N° 860 N° 8 N° 929 N° 930 N° 931 N° 932 N° 933 N° 934

N° 942 N° 943 N° 944 N° 945 N° 946 N° 947 N° 948 N° 949

N° 866 N° 867 N° 868 N° 869 N° 870 N° 871 N° 872 N° 873 N° 874 N° 875 N°

"I DON'T LIKE TO CALL THEM MY FANS BECAUSE THEY'RE MY FAMILY; THEY'RE THE ONLY REASON I'M ANYTHING. I LOVE MY FANS SO MUCH, I TRY TO DEVOTE ALL MY ATTENTION TO THEM, WHETHER IT'S ON SOCIAL MEDIA OR WHEN I SEE THEM IN PERSON. I SPEND AS MUCH TIME WITH THEM AS I CAN AND MAKE CONNECTIONS WITH THEM 'CAUSE THEY'RE PEOPLE."

jumped into my head and wrote a song through my thoughts, it was so weird."

Once the track was complete, late on a Wednesday evening (November 18, 2015, to be precise), Billie uploaded it to SoundCloud, indifferent to it getting lost in the noisy ether of the platform. In fact, the only reason she uploaded the track that night was because she needed a link to send to her dance teacher. "We were going to wait until Friday to put it out, and thought, 'Screw it. Let's just put it out now.' My dance teacher knew that I sang, so we recorded 'Ocean Eyes,' basing all of the production around contemporary and lyrical dance," said Billie. Her teacher was planning to use the song as part of a class recital. "I think of most of my songs that way—if you can't dance to a song, it's not a song."

The link went live, and soon the song became alive itself. Billie's friends started texting her about it. "Half my friends thought it was a joke. I remember specifically someone saying, 'Billie, this is ****.'"

The track started getting a lot of likes and listens. By the end of the night, Billie's future was carved in stone.

The next morning Billie went about her day as normal. "I was at Starbucks and Finneas called, like, 'Dude! Our song got 1,000 plays. We made it.' We were just so over the moon about it getting 1,000 plays. We were like, 'That's it. We've reached our goal.' We thought we were bosses. And then it just kept going. And then [music discovery website] Hillydilly found it and it went viral. I didn't realize how big it was getting until it had reached

LEFT AND PREVIOUS PAGE Billie brings the Chanel bling, New York, November 10, 2017.

BELOW Billie and Finneas perform at Glamour Magazine's prestigious Women of the Year Live event in New York, November 13, 2017.

50,000 plays. I haven't really processed it. It doesn't happen to everyone, and it's rare."

"Ocean Eyes" exploded everywhere. Within weeks Billie and Finneas were swamped with phone calls and meetings. The big break of the ocean's waves came when Apple Music's Beats 1 maestro and Zen-like tastemaker, Zane Lowe, gave Billie a digital shout-out. People were listening. "Billie has an ability to speak to her vulnerability in a way that represents it at its most creative," said Lowe. "She has a way of painting pictures that is universal—I can see them, but I'm blown away by how she paints them. An artist like Billie Eilish thinks in sounds, she thinks in colors, she thinks in visuals, she thinks in collaborations, she thinks in all kinds of different forms of creativity."

With Lowe's approval, Billie blew up. The success of "Ocean Eyes" not only gave the duo a springboard to stardom, it also showed their fans that they weren't some manicured and manufactured pop act with an unlimited budget. They had come straight from their bedrooms. They looked like you. Possibly even more dishevelled. Billie wasn't just a voice for

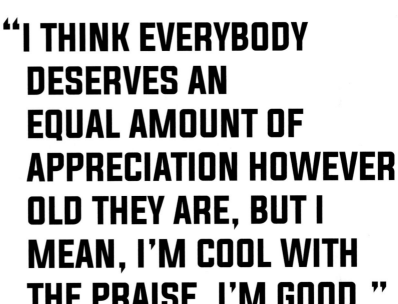

"I THINK EVERYBODY DESERVES AN EQUAL AMOUNT OF APPRECIATION HOWEVER OLD THEY ARE, BUT I MEAN, I'M COOL WITH THE PRAISE. I'M GOOD."

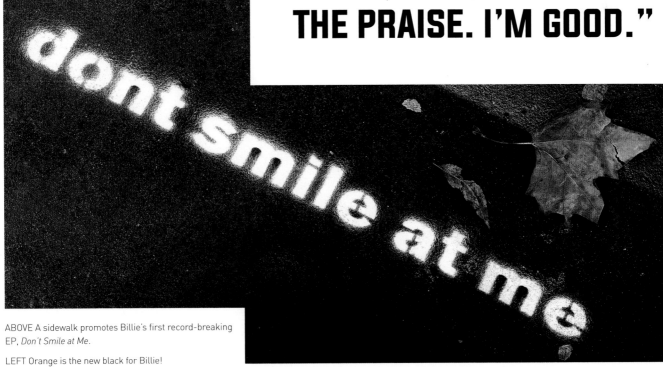

ABOVE A sidewalk promotes Billie's first record-breaking EP, *Don't Smile at Me*.

LEFT Orange is the new black for Billie!

fans her age—*she was one of them*. They had created a hit from their bedroom. If they could, anyone could. "When I was starting to make music, I thought I had to pay a bunch of people to do all my things professionally and that that would be the only way I would ever have any success," said Finneas. "It's really important for kids to not think that there's something intangible and out of reach for them. The truth is that you just have to make a song that people like. It was mixed and mastered by me and uploaded to SoundCloud. And that song saved our lives."

Six months later, in the summer of 2016, Billie signed with Darkroom, a boutique label in partnership with Interscope Records. Immediately, she and Finneas set to work putting together their first EP. After a few months of writing together, they already had more than enough songs—but which ones perfectly represented Billie's vision?

"WHEN WE ARE MAKING A SONG FOR BILLIE, I WANT IT TO RESONATE AND SPEAK THE TRUTH WITH HER, AND WANT IT TO BE A PIECE OF FABRIC SHE CAN WEAR." FINNEAS

TOP Blonde ambition prevails at UMG's Music is Universal Showcase, SXSW Festival, Austin, March 2017.

LEFT Billie rocks "Hotline Bling" on the ukulele at the Central Presbyterian Church, Austin, 16 March 2017.

OPPOSITE Wrapped in fake fur and leopard print, Billie dials in the style at the 34th Annual ASCAP Pop Music Awards, Los Angeles, 18 May 2017.

CHAPTER FOUR

FAR FROM HOME

"OCEAN EYES" TURNED BILLIE AND FINNEAS INTO NATIONAL CURIOSITIES. TOGETHER, THE SIBLING SONGWRITERS BEGAN BELTING OUT GEN-Z BANGERS FROM THEIR BEDROOM, BUILDING ON BILLIE'S REPUTATION FOR TOTAL CREATIVE FREEDOM, DISTINCTIVE FASHION CHOICES, AND A STUNNINGLY UNIQUE APPROACH TO VISUAL ARTISTRY

Billie was soon singled out as a dark-pop antihero, the voice of Gen Z, the pitch-perfect symbol of how the world feels right now. Not that she cared about that stuff. "I remember the first couple of times people called me the face of pop or whatever . . . it irked me. We think we have to label everything, but we don't." She simply calls her music "Billie Eilish music."

Nine months after the release of "Ocean Eyes" Billie birthed her debut EP, *Don't Smile At Me*, a nine-song collection of tracks she and Finneas had spent 18 months working on before Darkroom Records came aboard. But before the EP was scheduled for release, the family went on their first tour. Instead of it being a champagne-fuelled, five-star luxury hotel jaunt, conducted by private planes, the tour was a reminder of just how difficult life on the road can be for a fledging artist, regardless of public devotion. Billie hated the experience. Her struggles with her mental health returned, including depression and self-harm. It was to be the beginning of her darkest point, just as the world began its fixed stare.

The whole family—Billie, her parents, and brother—newly appointed tour manager Brian Marquis, and a friend helping out on the merchandise stand all shared a cramped van. Marquis had assigned a hotel budget of $100 a night for all six travellers. Naturally, Billie and her family shared a single room and, often, just the one bed. "It was miserable," she recalls. "Horrible

"I HAVE AN AMAZING JOB, DUDE. I REALLY DO. THE THINGS I GET TO DO IN MY CAREER HAVE JUST BEEN UNBELIEVABLE. CAN YOU BELIEVE THIS IS REAL?"

Motel 6s. Tiny little rooms. We took it slow on purpose, so it would be more impactful when we got to the venue—but we took it way slower than we needed to." As her dad Patrick remembers, "It was fun, sort of." At the start of the tour Patrick quit his job (making Barbie dolls), so he could concentrate on Billie's career full-time, becoming roadie-in-chief. He drove the van and taught himself how to prepare and operate stage lights. "I wanted to be a part of it because it's pretty darn cool," Patrick said of the time. "It felt like an endless limbo," Billie says of touring. "Like there was no end in sight. And, I mean, it's true, There really is no end in sight with touring."

Since Billie's first tour, the singer (and her family) have taken to the road on four more occasions: the *Where's My Mind* Tour (2018); the *1 by 1* Tour (2018–19); as the support act for Florence + The Machine (2018–19); the *When We All Fall Asleep* World Tour (2019); and in 2020, the *Where Do We Go?* World Tour. In 2018 Billie effectively played in every festival slot she could get her hands on—a career move that helped her grow her fanbase exponentially. Though, as was to be expected, with each new outing, Billie's tour crew expanded and

the buses got a bit bigger and better. "We basically upgraded to a bus that's way better for Billie and worse for everyone else," revealed Maggie. For the *When We All Fall Asleep* World Tour, Billie ensured that her tour manager Brian Marquis chartered an extra bus so she could take her friends from back home out on the road with her. "It cost a lot of money, and we can't even afford it," Billie said. "But I needed it for my mental health. I'm really trying hard to make touring as good as possible for me, because I want to love what I do. I don't *want* to be miserable. But when there are things that make you miserable . . . it's miserable!"

Once the first tour was complete, Billie and Finneas threw themselves back into completing the writing and recording sessions for the EP. Locked away in their bedroom writing and recording, it soon became evident that Billie's sound was developing into something fresh and strange. Naturally, she refused to define it. Many of the

TOP Billie gets in the Yuletide spirit at KROQ Acoustic Christmas event, the Forum, Inglewood, California, December 9, 2018.

LEFT Billie and YouTube star Kandee Johnson attend a VIP Party, Los Angeles, October 19, 2018.

OPPOSITE Billie rocks the alien-sweat-pants-and-hoodie look at NYLON's Annual Young Hollywood Party in Los Angeles.

songs from the EP were released as singles in the run-up to the EP. Initially considered a sleeper hit, *Don't Smile At Me* has since gone on to become a genreless modern classic. The videos for every song—including "Bellyache," "When the Party's Over," "Watch," and "COPYCAT," as well separate tracks "Bitches Broken Hearts" and "Lovely" with Khalid—have amassed huge views, now counting more than four billion. As you can tell by the eclectic release of music, from the haunting choral pop of "Ocean Eyes" to the bleak horror hip-hop of "Bad Guy" to the electropop of "Bellyache," Billie's music defies expectation and convention.

Released on August 11, 2017, *Don't Smile At Me* is that rare beauty—a collection of songs written by a self-made 16-year-old, drenched in swagger and confidence beyond those years, that sounds unlike anything else you've ever heard. It was all pure instinct too. "I always know what I want to do. So with that, I didn't even talk to anybody, I didn't ask anybody, I was like, 'Okay, this is the order of the songs, these are all the songs that are going to be on the EP, I want the EP cover to be me in red on a red ladder, in a yellow room, with a bunch of chains on. And the EP is called *Don't Smile at Me*. That's it. Boom. Bye.' And then the label were like, 'Okay.'"

Don't Smile At Me contains zero percent compromise. It is the sound of a visionary artist as nature intended:

no filler. Indeed, before Billie signed her record deal with Darkroom, the label invited her to relocate to a real studio and asked her to collaborate with other songwriters and producers. Billie reluctantly agreed but was quick to realize it went against everything she stood for. "I hated it so much. It was always these fifty-year-old men who'd written these 'big hit songs!' and then they're horrible at it. I'm like, 'You did this a hundred years ago. Ugh.' No one listened to me, because I was fourteen and a girl. But we made 'Ocean Eyes' without anyone involved—so why do I have to do this?"

> **"I COMPLETELY RECOGNIZE THE RESPONSIBILITY OF BEING A ROLE MODEL. BUT IT'S NOT GOING TO CHANGE THE WAY THAT I AM. I THINK INSTEAD OF CHANGING THE ART I MAKE, IT'S ABOUT LETTING EVERYONE KNOW THAT MY ART IS JUST MY WAY OF RELEASE."**

ABOVE Billie reaches out to her fans during KROQ's Acoustic Christmas at the Forum, Inglewood, California.

RIGHT Even on stage, Billie manages to create an intimate and introspective atmosphere.

DON'T SMILE AT ME: TRACKLIST

Billie refused and returned to her childhood bedroom, and she and Finneas finished the EP without any other interruptions. "I was just making songs with my brother," she said at the time. "Now it's like a thing: I'm this artist who's going against the whatever . . . I was just making what I wanted."

The EP's title is as brave as it is apt. Flying in the face of pop convention, rather than Billie fake smiling for the cameras, for the music industry, she instead flips the finger at the fame game and invites her fans to appreciate her realness. "I hate smiling. It makes me feel weak and powerless and small. I've always been like that; I don't smile in any pictures. If you look at my Instagram, I have a resting bitch face and I guess I just look sad all the time. But you know how when you're walking down the street and somebody smiles at you? You're forced to smile back, that's the polite response. It's like you have no control over it. If I don't smile back you're going to think I'm horrible. Maybe I am for thinking this, but whatever. And if you don't smile at me, we're good. You can go on with your day."

The success of *Don't Smile At Me* allowed Billie to feel confident in her ability to have complete creative freedom, away from the repressive arms of the industry. That desire for everything to be done her way was born, again, in the loving atmosphere of her family home, where she was free to be Billie. "I'm lucky to have a family that I like, and that likes me," she said. "The only reason I do what I do is because my parents didn't force me. If they'd said, 'Here's a guitar, here's a microphone, sing and write,' I would have been like, 'Goodbye! I'm going to go do drugs.'"

Billie's desire to be her own force of nature, at just 16, means that she is unlikely to be pushed around or forced to compromise her sound and vision in the future. And it's set the path for other aspiring musicians to follow. "What the hell would the point be if I was just creating something that somebody else wanted me to create, that I had no say in?" she stated. By challenging the normative expectations of what a female pop star can sound like, look like, and publicly say, Billie is changing the rules to favor the players, not the game. "I could easily just be like, 'You know what, you're going to pick out my clothes, someone else will come up with my video treatments, someone else will direct them, and I won't have anything to do with them,'" she said. "Someone else write my music, someone else produce it, and I won't say anything about it. Someone else run my Instagram. Everything could be easier if I wanted it to. But I'm not that kind of person and I'm not that kind of artist. And I'd rather die than be that kind of artist."

For example, how many 16-year-old artists choose to shoot a music video in which black ink pours from their eyes? On paper it must have sounded crazy, but it was essential for Billie to express the visions she saw in her mind. "I want to freak people out to an extent, so I put spiders in my mouth, I put them all over me. I put black liquid in my eyes and cry it out and drink it.

ABOVE Billie joins her fans at the Bonnaroo Arts and Music Festival in Manchester, Tennessee.

LEFT Taking care of business at the ASCAP Pop Awards, Los Angeles, May 18, 2017.

"I'M GREAT FRIENDS WITH MYSELF. ME AND ME GET ALONG REALLY WELL. I THINK I'M REALLY FUNNY SOMETIMES, I CAN HAVE A GOOD TIME ALONE AND I CAN MAKE MYSELF LAUGH, WHICH I THINK IS IMPORTANT. BUT I DON'T KNOW IF ANYONE KNOWS THEMSELVES FOR REAL. WE ONLY SEE A REFLECTED IMAGE OF OURSELVES IN PICTURES OR IN OTHER PEOPLE."

The stuff I'm thinking about right now and what I want to create is crazy. It's a challenge with myself, how can I freak people out more in an artistic way, that also looks dope?"

The video for "When the Party's Over" is a disturbing, bleak, and challenging pop music video, especially coming from someone under the age of 18. And yet, of course, it's a perfect representation of Billie's incredibly creative mind.

In the video, shot in one take, Billie (with dark blue hair) drinks from a glass of black ink. Seconds later, the ink starts leaking from her eyes and down her face. It's unsettling, but hypnotizing. And it's pure creation from Billie, who devised the direction. "I decided it was going to be a video and planned everything out like a director," Billie recalls of coming up with the idea. "I have this video of me . . . I went into my yard and told my Mom to pretend to be me. I made her go outside with a table, a glass, and the chair in the position exactly where I wanted it and I started filming and deciding how we shot it and everything." The video now has almost half a billion views.

Of course, Billie's journey to stardom, at such a relatively young age, hasn't all been paved with gold. Her struggle to find happiness, within herself and with others, while at the eye of a hurricane of fame, has dragged her down below the depths of her own mental wellbeing. "The last two years were kind of the worst mentally for me," she said. "I felt like nothing mattered. Every single thing was pointless. Not just in my life, but everything in the whole world. I was fully clinically depressed. I was a sixteen-year-old girl who was really unstable. All I can say, now I'm doing better, for anybody who isn't doing well, it will get better. Have hope. I did this . . . with fame riding on my shoulders. And I love fame! Being famous is great, but it was horrible for a year. Now I love what I do, and I'm me again. The good me. And I love the eyes on me."

RIGHT Fans use their phones to capture Billie's set at the Minneapolis Armory in June 2019.

BELOW Billie's long festival circuit tour takes to the stage at Music Midtown in Atlanta, Georgia.

NEXT PAGE Billie in portrait mode. Can you name the band t-shirt? (It's Wu-Tang-Clan!)

"PEOPLE ARE TERRIFIED OF ME, AND I WANT THEM TO BE." BILLIE

BELOW Billie wears a jewel-encrusted BILLIE mask at the 2019 iHeartRadio Music Festival in Las Vegas, September 21, 2019.

RIGHT Billie keeps it real in Beverly Hills!

MORE ME THAN I AM: BILLIE'S STYLE

BILLIE EILISH SOUNDS LIKE NO OTHER ARTIST IN THE WORLD. SHE DOESN'T LOOK LIKE ANY OTHER ARTIST IN THE WORLD EITHER, CHOOSING TO WEAR AN OUTRAGEOUSLY DIVERSE AND WONDERFULLY ECLECTIC RANGE OF CLOTHING AND BLING THAT SHOWS OFF HER UNIQUE APPROACH TO HER OWN ARTISTRY. TODAY, BILLIE IS AS MUCH A FASHION ICON AS SHE IS A MUSICAL ONE. AND THERE ARE SEVERAL GOOD REASONS WHY . . .

Close your eyes and think of Billie Eilish. What do you see? No doubt a neon-technicolored palette of swag of all sorts of sizes and shapes springs to mind. Say what you want about this dark-pop rebel, but she isn't dull or bland. This could be down to a condition called synaesthesia, a neurological phenomenon. Billie and Finneas both have it. Yet another blessing passed down through DNA. But what is it? Billie describes it best: "You think of a color when you see a word, or you smell something when you see a certain thing. So with songs and production and even clothing, when I'm making music and when I'm writing and singing, I kind of subconsciously imagine a color, or a landscape, or some type of visual element is in my head."

But, of course, it isn't just Billie's synaesthesia that defines her fashion choices. Fashion is her armour too. It protects her from the slings and arrows of the world. "Fashion and clothing have always been my safety blanket, my guard, and if I am wearing something that I don't want to be wearing, or mentally or physically uncomfortable with, I am completely not me. It just feels so wrong and so clothing is really the way that I am— it's more me than I am."

"MY WHOLE PERSONALITY IS BASED OFF MY CLOTHES AND WHAT I'M WEARING THAT DAY. I'LL HAVE A DIFFERENT PERSONALITY FOR A DIFFERENT OUTFIT SOMETIMES. IT'S THE FIRST THING THAT MATTERS IN EVERY DAY OF MY LIFE. EVERYWHERE I GO, EVERYTHING I DO. EVERYTHING."

Ever since Billie was a child, clothing has played an integral part of her day. She dressed her own way before she became famous. Her unique dress sense is a symbol that represents Billie's desire for pure creative freedom: she dresses how she wants, regardless of how others may perceive those choices. "I like being able to express myself with clothing. I don't mind being judged if someone doesn't like what I wear. I am okay with it. Each day I try to wear stuff that I haven't worn before or I'll wear a part of an outfit in a different way. I will draw on my shoes, turn my shirt inside out, or cut up my pants. I like mixing thrift-store clothing with brand names." Indeed, she describes her style as "super-cheap meets fancy."

Billie's fashion, along with her music videos, are the icon's way of expressing how she feels on the inside, as well how she refuses to look the way you would expect someone like her to look. Some days she dresses in all black, some days it's all camouflage, and some days it's all neon. "Clothing and visual art is the most important for me and always has been," she has said. "I think of myself, in my head, more of a visual artist than anything else. Of course music is what I do, I sing and whatever, but everything I do is my idea. All the videos I have are my idea. I have a specific thing that I want for each thing that I make, and I usually have it when I make it."

"I HAVE ALWAYS BEEN A PERSON THAT WANTS TO DRESS LOUD. I ALWAYS WANTED TO LOOK LOUD, I'VE ALWAYS WANTED PEOPLE TO LOOK AT ME, I'VE ALWAYS WANTED PEOPLE TO NOTICE ME. AND THAT'S BEEN A PART OF ME SINCE BEFORE ANY OF THE FAME . . . HAPPENED."

ABOVE A style icon for a new century. Billie goes Gucci in Los Angeles, November 2, 2019.

LEFT Billie dresses in something special for her Spotify Presents show.

RIGHT Billie covered in Chanel's haute couture in New York.

CHAPTER FIVE:

PHENOM

BEFORE BILLIE TURNED 17 IN DECEMBER 2018, SHE HAD ACCOMPLISHED PRETTY MUCH EVERYTHING REQUIRED OF A POPSTAR SUPER ICON. SHE HAD BUILT HER EMPIRE ORGANICALLY FROM THE CONFINES OF HER TINY BEDROOM. BEFORE SHE EVEN RELEASED THE GROUNDBREAKING *WHEN WE FALL ASLEEP, WHERE DO WE GO?*, BILLIE HAD CLOCKED UP MORE THAN A BILLION STREAMS ON DIGITAL PLATFORMS. WITH THE ALBUM'S RELEASE, HOWEVER, SHE HAD TRULY ARRIVED. SHE BECAME THE YOUNGEST-EVER FEMALE SOLO ACT TO GO STRAIGHT TO NUMBER 1 IN THE US AND UK, AND THE FIRST NUMBER 1 ARTIST TO BE BORN THIS MILLENNIUM. IT'S BILLIE'S WORLD NOW, AND SHE'S NOT GIVING IT BACK.

To Billie, what was more important than all the accolades, awards, praise, and stellar reviews of *When We Fall Asleep, Where Do We Go?* was the simple fact that the album actually got made. And that she considered it to be good. "I just love what I've created, which is rare. I'm very happy with it," Billie revealed. "We've worked on it for a really long time and it was really kind of miserable to work on it."

Indeed, unlike the sessions for *Don't Smile At Me,* recorded at home, the production sessions for the LP were done on the road during Billie's exhausting *Where's My Mind* and *1 by 1* headline tours, on the supporting tour with Florence + The Machine, and between appearances at pretty much all the stops on the summer festival circuit in Europe and the US. These live dates took their toll on the artist and her producer, with Finneas setting up a makeshift studio in hotel rooms and working for six

ABOVE Billie poses before her gig at the German music and art festival MS Dockville in Hamburg.

LEFT Billie in a hi-vis vest is both seen and heard at the Swiss Music Awards 2019 in Luzern, Switzerland.

hours on the production before playing a show, day in day out. For Billie, there was a real danger that the album would never see the light of day.

As it turned out, it was the constant and exhausting touring of 2018 that helped infuse the album with more flavors. "Touring has taught me and my brother a lot about thinking things like, 'What is fun to perform? What is fun to jump around the stage to? What do audiences like the most? What is the best? What is the craziest?'" Due to overwhelming demand for Billie to be everywhere, and with more than a hundred shows racked up in 2018, she and Finneas had the opportunity to road-test songs, to work out what kind of album they wanted to make, knowing that they would then have to take it on tour for the next 18 months. "Basically, for this album, we're making music that's going to be crazy to do live," said Billie. "We're just going to go hard. But we're also making [music] to cry to. Everything. That's where I come from, so that's what I want." Due to her strained relationship with touring, the last thing she wants to do is traipse around the world not feeling her own music and lying to her fans. She wants them on their feet, dancing around, having the time of their lives. "I want to be jumping around and jumping on people and breaking people's arms and stuff. All I want is for my shows to be crazy and full of mosh pits and people

TOP Fans as far afield as Moscow, Russia, can't wait to see Billie perform.

ABOVE Catching serious air at Coachella in April 2019.

LEFT Due to her increased UK popularity, Billie had to be moved to a bigger stage at Glastonbury 2019.

"FAME IS LIKE A MEDICATION. BUT IT DOESN'T MAKE ME FEEL BETTER." BILLIE

enjoying themselves. I don't want to make crazy feel-good music that has no meaning. Right now, I feel like I'm making music that's going to be so fun to do live. That's what I've learned from being on tour. What do I like the most and what do they like the most?"

Recorded between May and December 2018, *When We Fall Asleep, Where Do We Go?* was a torturous first record to birth, Billie herself admitted. This was in part due to the weight of expectation that Finneas and she felt as primary songwriters, following the critical and commercial acclaim they received for 2018's *Don't Smile At Me.* The world was waiting for them to mess up. "People are always like, 'Yeah she's changing for fame.' And I'm like, 'No bro. I'm just changing. I'm . . . sixteen. Dude, the difference between me at sixteen and me at fourteen is a whole different person, and that would be that way no matter what . . . I was doing with my life. My music tastes are going to change no matter

what. My style's going to change. I'm going to change. Everything around me is going to change. Doesn't matter about fame or whatever. 'She's changing for fame. The fame is getting to her.' Bro, shut . . . up. Obviously I'm changing. Because we all do, so get off [me]."

Naturally, Billie and Finneas delivered the record they wanted to make. And it is a modern masterpiece.

> **"YOU DON'T HAVE TO BE IN LOVE WITH SOMEONE TO WRITE A SONG ABOUT BEING IN LOVE WITH SOMEONE. YOU DON'T HAVE TO HATE SOMEBODY TO WRITE A SONG ABOUT HATING SOMEBODY. YOU DON'T HAVE TO KILL PEOPLE TO WRITE A SONG ABOUT KILLING PEOPLE. I'M NOT GOING TO KILL PEOPLE, SO I'M JUST GOING TO BECOME ANOTHER CHARACTER."**

TOP The iconic Troubadour venue gears up to host Billie in 2019.

ABOVE Ahead of her debut album release, Billie already owns the stage.

RIGHT Billie takes a knee during a 2019 performance in Chicago.

When writing sessions began for the album, which was recorded in their childhood bedroom and makeshift studio in Highland Park, the pair worked in short, 45-minute sessions during the day, and then all night long, throwing lyrics and hooks at each other. Billie would record her vocals while lying on Finneas's bed. "Most people need to stand and open their diaphragms, but Billie sounds amazing just slumped on the bed. I just want Billie's voice to sound like Billie's voice. Her voice is like a Stradivarius violin—it's so beautiful I don't have to do anything." They kept a progress chart scribbled on Finneas's wall, right above where they used to mark their heights as children.

The album's dark tone, conversational lyrics, vocal delivery, and fusion of several disparate genres of music—EDM, trap, jazz, electropop, hip-hop—set

LEFT Jumping for joy at the Lollapalooza music festival in Stockholm, Sweden.

RIGHT Fans show the love at Marymoor Park in Redmond, Washington, June 2, 2019.

BELOW Billie knocks it out the park at the 2019 iHeartRadio Music Festival at Las Vegas Festival Grounds.

"I JUST REALLY WANT TO GET MUSIC OUT AND TOUR AND GO PLACES I'VE NEVER BEEN, AND JUST DO MORE VIDEOS. I LOVE PHOTOGRAPHY AND VIDEOGRAPHY AND SO I REALLY WANT TO DIRECT VIDEOS WHEN I CAN. I WANT TO HAVE A FASHION LINE AT SOME POINT VERY SOON."

tongues wagging, but it was the significance of the long title that had people wondering. For Billie, dreams mean something more than just your brain compartmentalizing a day's events. They are voyages of discovery. "I mean, where . . . do we go?!" she said. "Dreams are a really intense part of my life. I'll go through a month where I'll have the same nightmare every single night—a dream that's so bad that the whole day is off, or a dream that's so good that none of it's true."

Billie has been haunted by bad dreams since she was young. It's her dreams that inform her lyrics, her visual state, and all of it is born out of her underlying anxiety and depression about herself and the world. The paradox of Billie's dreams is that they keep her awake and yet give her the dark visual ammunition that drips and leaks into her lyrics. Her unconscious mind flavors her waking thoughts. "It takes me hours to fall asleep. I only last year started having sleep paralysis, but I would say that might be one of the worst things in the whole world. I just have been

WHEN YOU FALL ASLEEP, WHERE DO WE GO?: THE TRACKLIST

1. "!!!!!!!" 2. "BAD GUY" 3. "XANNY"
4. "YOU SHOULD SEE ME IN A CROWN"
5. "ALL THE GOOD GIRLS GO TO HELL"
6. "WISH YOU WERE GAY" 7. "WHEN THE PARTY'S OVER"
8. "8" 9. "MY STRANGE ADDICTION" 10. "BURY A FRIEND"
11. "ILOMILO" 12. "LISTEN BEFORE I GO"
13. "I LOVE YOU" 14. "GOODBYE"

ABOVE Billie wins New Artist of the Year award at the 2019 American Music Awards in Los Angeles. It's her first major

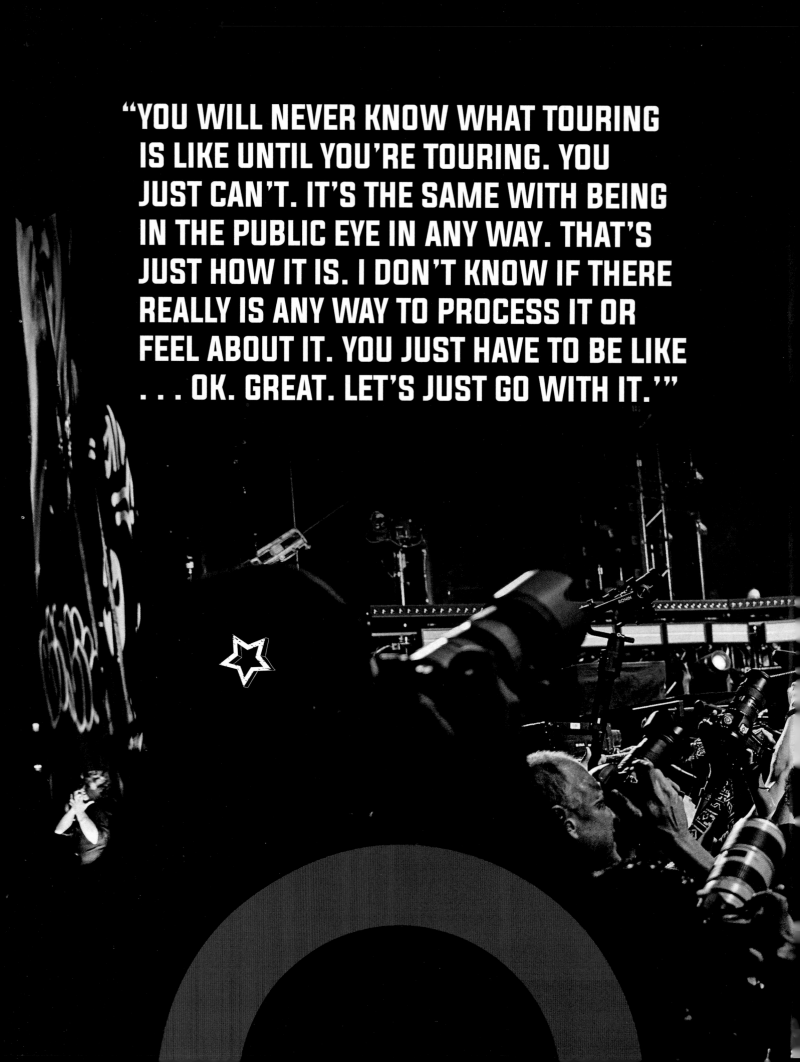

"YOU WILL NEVER KNOW WHAT TOURING IS LIKE UNTIL YOU'RE TOURING. YOU JUST CAN'T. IT'S THE SAME WITH BEING IN THE PUBLIC EYE IN ANY WAY. THAT'S JUST HOW IT IS. I DON'T KNOW IF THERE REALLY IS ANY WAY TO PROCESS IT OR FEEL ABOUT IT. YOU JUST HAVE TO BE LIKE . . . OK. GREAT. LET'S JUST GO WITH IT.'"